Wimbledc

The Changing Face of Worple Road

by
Alan Little
Honorary Librarian
Wimbledon Lawn Tennis Museum

Wimbledon Lawn Tennis Museum
London
2015

The Worple Road ground was opened in late May, 1870 and a few weeks later the Croquet Championships were held. Most of the leading players took part and are seen in front of the new Club Pavilion. From left to right: **J.H. Walsh** *(Hon. Treasurer),* **S.H.C. Maddock** *(Hon. Secretary), H. Jones,* **J.H. Hale**, *W.H. Peel (seated on ground), Rev. A. C Pearson, Rev. J.I. Heath, Major Lane,* **W.J. Whitmore**, *G. Nicol, G.C. Joad, E.C. Haines,* **Rev. A. Law**, *A. Lillie (standing), Rev. J.B. Riley (seated), W.R.D. Maycock (seated on ground), G.A. Muntz, J.D. Heath (Club Champion) and G.R. Elsmie. The five names in bold were members of the founding Committee in 1868 (Capt. R.F. Dalton was absent).*

Ever since 1877, The Lawn Tennis Championships have been staged annually at Wimbledon, first at the ground just off Worple Road until 1921, and then at the present Church Road ground, from 1922 to date.

Over this period the tournament has developed from the garden party atmosphere, watched by a few hundred spectators, to a highly professional event, attracting an attendance of approaching half a million and through the press, radio and television a following of many millions throughout the world.

The story began nine years earlier, when on the 23rd July 1868, six gentlemen, John Walsh, Capt. R.F. Dalton, J. Hinde Hale, Reverend A. Law, S.H. Clarke Maddock and Walter Jones Whitmore, met in the offices of 'The Field', the Country Gentlemen's Newspaper, at 346 Strand in London and founded the 'All England Croquet Club'.

This provisional committee agreed Walsh would be Chairman, Whitmore, Hon. Secretary and Maddock, Hon. Treasurer, also that the annual subscription be set at one guinea.

A few weeks later the Committee set about the task of securing a ground, but this was far from easy. Many sites around London were inspected but none were suitable, either because of location, size or cost.

The 1869 croquet season came and went, with the Club still without a ground. However, the Committee were not idle and in July of that year organised the first Croquet Championships on a cricket ground at Crystal Palace. G.C. Joad became the Champion and W.H. Peel, Club Champion. Later in the year another tournament was held at Eastbourne.

On 24th September the Committee considered an offer from Mr. Albert Dixon, a Wimbledon solicitor, to let the Club four acres of land at Wimbledon, situated between Worple Road and the London and South Western Railway, about half a mile west of Wimbledon station, for three years at an annual rent of £50 for the first year, £75 for the second year and £100 for the third year. In those days Wimbledon, a rural town in the County of Surrey, must have seemed a far cry from London where the Club meetings took place. Worple Road was little more than a cart-track. Bordering the ground on the south-west side was the Southdown dairy farm and on the opposite side was a Brick Field, soon to become Sycamore Builder's Works.

There was a difference of opinion as to whether the offer should be accepted, with some of the Committee thinking that the finances of the Club would not justify the expense required for levelling, turfing, draining and fencing the ground. However, a group of enthusiastic members subscribed a sum of £600 between them as a 'donation fund' and with this behind them, the Committee finally decided to go ahead on 15th October.

By mid-December, a tender of £425 was accepted to lay out the new ground. This was quite a challenge as the fall of the ground was 14 feet in one direction and 9 feet in the other. However, within six months the task was completed, with the result being the ground was laid out in three terraces, each containing four full-sized croquet lawns.

The ground was opened in late May 1870 and a month later the competitors at the second Croquet Championships were able to use the facilities of the newly built Pavilion. The number of new members accepted by the Committee increased dramatically and all seemed well for a few years, but by the time 1874 came around the interest in croquet had waned and so had the finances of the Club.

Coinciding with this, the new game of Lawn Tennis, just introduced to the public by Major Walter Clopton Wingfield, was sweeping the country and the Committee, looking to revive the fortunes of the Club, announced on 25th February 1875 that one croquet lawn would be set apart for the playing of Lawn Tennis and Badminton.

Lawn Tennis and Croquet had nothing in common apart from the playing surface of cut lawn, but the Victorians were eager to seize on a pursuit which brought healthy and energetic competition.

In May 1875 the Marylebone Cricket Club took a hand in the affairs of Lawn Tennis and issued the first official set of laws. These had been laid down following a meeting of all interested parties and favoured the Wingfield hour-glass shaped court, where the distance between the posts was less than the baseline. Another feature was the scoring up to 15 points, as used in Rackets. The Club was content to abide by these laws for the time being and enthusiastically arranged for the players to hire balls and to provide lockers for their gear.

Reginald Gray from Bermuda was one of four men reputed to have played the very first game of lawn tennis on the ground early that summer. The same season, while studying in London, Gray won the Croquet Championship.

Support for the game grew quickly and by 1876 had gone some of the way to replacing croquet at the ground, so much so that an entire terrace of four lawns was made over to lawn tennis. Further recognition of the game came on 14th April 1877 when the Club changed its title to the 'All England Croquet and Lawn Tennis Club'.

On 2nd June the Committee, acting on a proposal by John Walsh, came to the momentous decision that 'A public meeting be held on 9th July and following days to compete for the Championship of Lawn Tennis and that a sub-committee of Messrs. J. Marshall, Henry Jones (Cavendish) and C.G. Heathcote be appointed to draw up the rules for its management'.

Above: An artist's impression of the first Lawn Tennis Championships in 1877. The ground is in three tiers divided by the four croquet summer houses. In the middle distance is the Pavilion, while on the extreme right is the railway line. Below: One of the two movable grandstands provided by F.H. Ayres in 1880. The Company were allowed to keep half the takings.

Having only just five and a half weeks at their disposal, the sub-committee had no time to waste. They immediately set about the general organisation of the meeting and producing a new set of laws, ignoring in most cases the M.C.C. code.

The matches were scheduled for Monday 9th July through to the Thursday and then miss the Friday and Saturday, so as not to clash with the Eton v. Harrow cricket match at Lords. The final was arranged for the Monday but rain prevented play and then was postponed until the following Thursday. Henry Jones was appointed Referee.

Twenty-two players entered The Championship, which was a Gentlemen's Singles event only. Spencer Gore, an old Harrovian and rackets player, became the first champion, defeating William Marshall in the final, 6-1 6-2 6-4, winning the first prize, value 12 guineas, plus a silver Challenge Cup, value 25 guineas, presented by the proprietors of 'The Field'.

The Club now entered a period of prosperity, when the number of spectators at The Championships increased each year. To cater for the upsurge in these numbers, two movable grandstands were provided in 1880 by F.H. Ayres for spectators to watch the expected important matches, staged on one of the courts in the middle of the ground. There is little doubt that this arrangement led to the idea of a permanent Centre Court, and a year later at the meeting, temporary stands were erected on three sides of the combined No.6 and No.7 Court to form the Centre Court.

In 1882 lawn tennis became very popular at the Club and gradually the croquet players felt their game was being squeezed out. Feeling ran high between the rival sections and this culminated on the 4th December when the title of the Club was changed to just 'The All England Lawn Tennis Club'. Croquet was not seen again at the Club for another 14 years.

A milestone occurred in 1884 when the Championship programme was extended to include a Ladies' Singles and a Gentlemen's Doubles Championship. Also that year the stand alongside the Centre Court was made a permanent structure, likewise a year later when the two ends of the court were similarly bounded.

The eighties were exciting times at the Club with the presence of the Renshaw twins, Ernest and William, particularly the latter who won the Gentlemen's singles title no less than seven times, during which period he transformed lawn tennis from a pastime to a competitive sport.

The nineties started well, with the Baddeley twins, Herbert and Wilfred, and Joshua Pim being the heroes of the time but gradually Club receipts dwindled as applications for membership and the sale of Championship tickets fell. Indeed in 1895 the meeting actually made a loss of £33. Part of the solution was to

These two remarkable photographs show what Wimbledon was like 120 years ago in 1883. The Centre Court was bordered on three sides by temporary wooden stands (C in front, A to the left and B behind the camera), which were dismantled after each Championship and stored away in sheds until the following year. The stands were made permanent structures in 1885 and 1886. The right side of the court, where spectators are sitting on chairs and benches, became the Uncovered Stand D. Two of the croquet summer houses may be seen and in the distance, on the right, are Nos. 6 and 7 Courts and the boundary fence next to the railway. (Players – J.E. & W.C. Renshaw v. C.M. & J.S. Clark – friendly).

invite the croquet players back and this was achieved in sufficient numbers for the Club to be thankful for their modest subscriptions.

The Croquet Championships were revived in 1897 but that was the year when the legendary Doherty brothers started their domination of The Championships, which was to last well into the Edwardian era. The Club and The Championships never looked back.

As a gesture to the croquet players the Club title was amended on 2nd December 1899 to the 'All England Lawn Tennis and Croquet Club', which still persists today. The upsurge in the croquet section did not last long and after the 1904 Championships the game disappeared once again from the lawns.

From the turn of the century The Championships assumed an international character when the number of foreign competitors increased annually, not just from nearby European countries but from far away places such as Argentina, Australia, New Zealand, South Africa and the United States. Also, Davis Cup ties were staged at the ground for the first time. All this encouraged more spectators than ever to visit the ground.

In 1906 the three Centre Court Covered Stands were demolished and rebuilt, allowing spectators more viewing space to see the rising stars of the game, with May Sutton from the United States and Norman Brookes from Australia leading the way and becoming the first overseas singles champions. Until this time, The Championships were completely the domain of the British.

British Royalty recognised The Championships for the first time in 1907 when the Prince and Princess of Wales attended the ground. The same day the Prince accepted the Presidency of the Club.

Over the next few years the Club made considerable improvements to the ground, including better toilet facilities, renovation of all paths, repairs to boundary fences and the upgrading of the drainage systems. In 1909 the Centre Court Covered Stand B was completely rebuilt, nine feet nearer the baseline of the court to increase the capacity by 500 seats.

The demand for Centre Court seats persisted and in 1913 the Covered Stand C was renewed but, limited to some degree in space, gave only another 400 seats. A year later, at great expense, Covered Stand A was replaced with a much larger building, which provided a continuous structure with the other two stands. This increased the court capacity from 2,300 to 3,500 seats. A feature of this new Stand was the underneath passageway, which overlooked two outside courts.

But all this new provision still fell short of what was required by the public to be able to watch the great players perform. Four times champion Anthony Wilding of New Zealand had a tremendous following, which created never ending queues and congestion.

The Centre Court in 1892. Covered Stand C is in the distance, with Uncovered Stand D on the right. Out of sight to the left is Covered Stand A and behind the camera is Covered Stand B. The formally dressed spectators in the foreground have plenty of space at their disposal as Stand B is set well back from the court. Note the Umpire is sitting in a chair, mounted on a table. Umpire's chairs did not appear until around 1896. (Players – E.W. Lewis & J. Pim).

In a desperate effort to alleviate the situation further, the Club purchased two houses adjoining the ground for conversion into dressing rooms and offices, and the gardens into a tea lawn. But it was to no avail – the ground was too small. When 6,000 people were present, the scene was described as 'very congested' and when the figure reached 7,500, the ground was 'packed to suffocation'.

For some time the Committee had discussed moving to larger premises, but any thoughts that way were obviously put aside at the start of the First World War. With the conflict over, The Championships resumed in 1919. The demand for tickets was quite unprecedented as Frenchwoman Suzanne Lenglen and Bill Tilden of the United States took centre stage. As a guide the number of reserved seats, which were available to the public for the whole duration of a meeting, was 500 and these were more than ten times over subscribed. Another problem was the inadequate space available to park the ever increasing number of motor vehicles at the Club entrance and surrounding streets.

Towards the end of 1919 the Club searched locally for a new ground and at the turn of the year was successful in acquiring sufficient land at Wimbledon Park. In the spring of 1920, the $13^{1}/_{4}$ acre ground was purchased and later plans put into action to lay out the site and build a magnificent new Centre Court stadium, having approximately three times the seating capacity as Worple Road. So it was, and in June 1922 the Church Road ground, as it became known, took over the responsibility of staging The Championships.

Epilogue
Sale of Ground
During July 1922 the freehold of the Worple Road ground, and the adjoining residences at No.108 and No.110 Worple Road, were put up for sale by the agents, Marler and Marler of Sloane Street, London, SW1. On the 1st October 1923 the ground was sold for £4,000 to the Girl's Public Day School Trust (Wimbledon High School for Girls), who are still the owners. The ground was secured as an open space for all time, and is still used as a playing field. The two houses, No.108 and No.110, were sold to other buyers for £1,000 and £900 respectively. Both were demolished many years ago.

Pony Roller
In 1871 John Walsh offered to present his pony roller to the Club on condition that his daughter be made a life member. The Committee accepted this offer and the roller remained on the Centre Court at Worple Road until being moved to the Church Road ground in 1922. Initially the roller was placed on

The two photographs show the layout of the Centre Court in 1900. Above: Covered Stand A, on the left, and Covered Stand C were installed in 1884 and 1885, respectively. Both, together with Covered Stand B (behind camera) were completely replaced by 1906. In the background of Stand A can be seen the buildings, which earlier housed the two covered courts. Below: On the right is Uncovered Stand D, erected in 1886 but rebuilt in 1904. (Players – Miss C. Cooper v. Mrs. B. Hillyard and R.F. Doherty v. S.H. Smith).

the Centre Court but was moved in 1924 to the newly opened No.1 Court. In 1986, the roller was moved to the Wimbledon Lawn Tennis Museum but in 2005 was resited, adjacent to the south-west entrance to No.1 Court.

Croquet

Croquet was not played at the Worple Road ground after the 1904 season. When the Club moved to the present Church Road ground in 1922 no provision was made for the game, but in 1953 matches were played. In 1957 a lawn was laid down but this is not full size and competitive play is restricted to Club tournaments. In 1960 the Club Championship was revived together with a handicap event.

Use of Stands

Late in 1922 materials were taken from the Worple Road Centre Court stands and were used to construct the new No.2 Court stands at the Church Road ground. These stands were demolished in 1932 and replaced by a concrete structure.

New Entrance Gates

On 31st May 1935 new gates at the entrance to the Worple Road ground were formally opened by Lord Ashcombe, the Lord Lieutenant of Surrey, in the presence of All England Lawn Tennis Club officials and other local dignitaries. A very notable lady present was Miss Lottie Dod, the winner of the singles five times between 1887 and 1893. The funds for the gates were raised by public subscription and amounted to over £1,000. In addition to the gates, a fountain was erected just inside the entrance to commemorate the Jubilee of King George V.

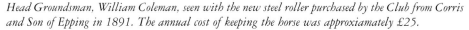

Head Groundsman, William Coleman, seen with the new steel roller purchased by the Club from Corris and Son of Epping in 1891. The annual cost of keeping the horse was approxiamately £25.

12

The following pages list year by year the changes that occurred at the All England Lawn Tennis Club's ground at Worple Road, Wimbledon from 1869 to 1921.

1868
The 'All England Croquet Club' was formed on 23rd July when six gentlemen, John H. Walsh (Chairman), Capt. R.F. Dalton, J. Hinde Hale, Revd. A. Law, S.H. Clarke Maddock and Walter Jones Whitmore met in the offices of Herbert Cox, the publisher of 'The Field' at 346 Strand, in London. Whitmore was elected Hon. Secretary and Maddock, Hon. Treasurer.

The annual subscription to the Club for Lady or Gentleman was fixed at one guinea, Husband and Wife at £1.11s.6d.

1869
In October, a ground of four acres at Wimbledon, between Worple Road and the London and South Western Railway, was rented for a period of three years at an annual rent of £50, £75 and £100. The ground was rectangular in shape, approximately 316 feet on both narrow sides and 554 feet and 570 feet on the long sides.

An agreement was made with the London and South Western Railway for a gateway and access from the pathway to Wimbledon Station at a rent of £1 a year. (Raised to £1.5s.0d. in 1885.)

1870
At a cost of £425 the ground was laid out in three terraces, each containing four full-sized croquet lawns. The ground was opened in late May.

Fencing around the ground was provided.

A small Pavilion containing a Gentlemen's and Ladies' Rooms and Club Room was built.

Croquet Championships held at the ground for the first time.

Four summer houses were built.

1871
The value of the Club ground was estimated to be worth £2,500.

1872
The Secretary, John Walsh, presented his pony roller to the Club and sold them his pony for £23.

1873
The lease on the Worple Road ground was renewed for a further ten years at £100 a year.

1875
Lawn Tennis was first played at the Club, when one lawn was set aside for the purpose.

1876
An entire terrace of four lawns was made over to lawn tennis.

1906: Above: The non-Championship Ladies' doubles final is being played on No.4 Court, which was situated between the Tea Lawn and No. 6 Court, behind the Centre Court Covered Stand C. (Players – Miss A.M. Morton & Mrs. C. Sterry v. Mrs. B. Hillyard & Miss M. Sutton). Middle: Tea is being taken with Centre Court Covered Stands C (left) and A in the background. The main board showing who was playing on which court is seen attached to Stand A (Wednesday 27th June). Below: A long line of varied cars in Worple Road await their passengers to return from the day's play.

1877

The title of the Club was changed to 'The All England Croquet and Lawn Tennis Club'.

The first Lawn Tennis Championships for Gentlemen's Singles only was staged on 9th-12th and 19th July. A sub-Committee of three, Charles Gilbert Heathcote, Henry Jones and Julian Marshall, were appointed to draw up rules for its management. They also laid down a new set of laws for the game. The court was rectangular, 78 feet by 27 feet, with the service line 26 feet from the net. The height of the net was 5 feet at the posts and 3 feet 3 inches at the centre. Tennis scoring was used. The matches the best of five sets, without advantage, except in the final set. The diameter of the balls was between $2^{1}/_{4}$ and $2^{5}/_{8}$ inches and the weight between $1^{1}/_{4}$ and $1^{1}/_{2}$ ounces.

Twelve courts were available for play. The number of spectators who attended is not recorded but at the final, staged on the lowest terrace by the railway, some 200 people were present. A selected few, about 30 in number were accommodated with seats in a stand of three tiers, erected for the occasion.

1878

The courts were stated to be in excellent condition following levelling during the winter.

1879

The Committee rejected the suggestion to stage a Ladies' Singles Championship.

1880

Two movable stands were provided by F.H. Ayres, for spectators to watch the expected important matches on a court in the middle of the ground. This idea was the beginning of a Centre Court being established.

The first scoring board was introduced because the noise of passing trains often made the calling of the umpire inaudible.

Additional dressing rooms were made available by renting the three upper rooms of the Roller Skating Rink building, at the rear of the Pavilion, at £26 per annum.

1881

Temporary wooden Covered Stands were erected on the north-west, south-west and north-east sides of a Centre Court and designated as A, B and C respectively. During the winter months the stands were dismantled and stored away in a special shed. The cost of the stands and shed was £350 and £65 respectively, and a further £70 was expended each year erecting and dismantling the stands (including hire of the awnings).
To give spectators more room during The Championships, the No. 1 Court in front of the Pavilion was dispensed with, leaving ten courts available for play. The distribution of the courts on the three terraces for all future meetings was: highest – Nos.1 to 3 Courts, middle – Centre Court and No. 4 and 5 Courts, lowest – Nos. 6 to 9 Courts.

The Club purchased the freehold of the ground for £3,000 - £500 down and the balance spread over seven years at 4%.

1882

The title of the Club was changed to the 'All England Lawn Tennis Club'.

The levelling and reclaiming of ground at each end of the three terraces enlarged the actual extent of the ground by about 30 feet.

Croquet ceased on the ground at the end of the season.

1883
A new horse and heavy roller, ropes and posts for enclosing the grounds on match days and a new cooking range were purchased.

1884
Centre Court Covered Stand A was made a permanent structure.

A new Refreshment Bar was erected in lieu of a hired tent.

Ladies' Singles and Gentlemen's Doubles Championships were added to the programme.

1885
Centre Court Covered Stands B and C were made permanent structures at the cost of approximately £150.

The first tarpaulin for the Centre Court was hired at the cost of £8.

1886
Improvements were made to the three Centre Court Covered Stands A, B and C. Part of Stand B was partitioned off for the Stewards and Press. On the south-east side of the Centre Court five-raised tiers were built to provide free viewing for over 500 spectators. (This uncovered structure became Stand D). The total cost of the work carried out on the stands amounted to approximately £200.

Stop nets, eight feet high, were placed at the rear of the courts.

Refreshments were served in the Pavilion.

1887
Over £260 was spent on improvements to the three Covered Stands.

1888
The appearance of the ground was improved by the erection of a new Entrance Gate.

Sunday play was allowed on the ground for the first time.

1889
The planting of shrubs and the laying out of flowerbeds gave a more picturesque appearance to the ground.

The drainage of the lawns was considerably improved.

The stands and other erections were re-painted in a more cheerful colour, while the stables were removed to a more convenient position.

The exterior of the Pavilion was beautified by an ornamental paling and the interior was papered and painted.

Layout of the ground for The Championships in 1907

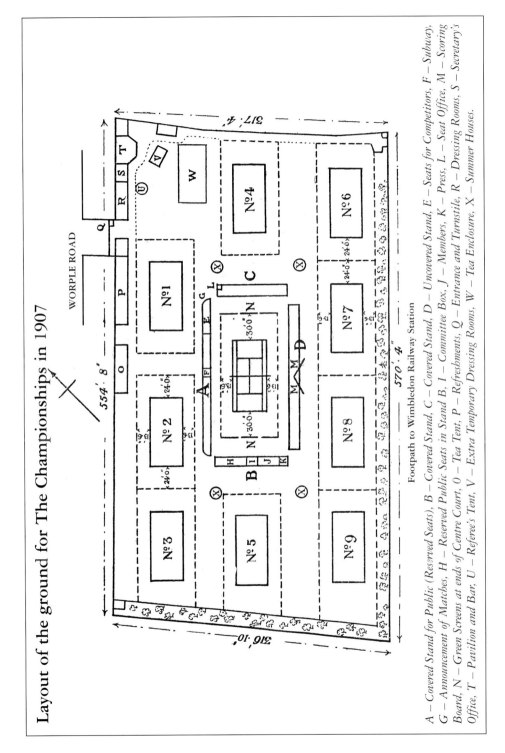

A – Covered Stand for Public (Reserved Seats), B – Covered Stand, C – Covered Stand, D – Uncovered Stand, E – Seats for Competitors, F – Subway, G – Announcement of Matches, H – Reserved Public Seats in Stand B, I – Committee Box, J – Members, K – Press, L – Seat Office, M – Scoring Board, N – Green Screens at ends of Centre Court, O – Tea Tent, P – Refreshments, Q – Entrance and Turnstile, R – Dressing Rooms, S – Secretary's Office, T – Pavilion and Bar, U – Referee's Tent, V – Extra Temporary Dressing Rooms, W – Tea Enclosure, X – Summer Houses.

Above left: A very congested Tea Lawn in 1905. Full waitress service and no one in sight without a hat. Right: 1908 and not a seat to spare in the Uncovered Stand D, on the railway side of the Centre Court. Below left: The Centre Court in 1908 showing Covered Stands A (left) and C, which had been rebuilt in 1906. Note the pony roller in the corner of the court. Right: 1911. The first tent-like cover installed on the Centre Court allowed the rainwater to run into drains at the two sides of the court.

1890

A new tarpaulin was purchased for the Centre Court at a cost of £60.

1891

The Committee were concerned that the arrangement of renting the upper dressing rooms of the premises adjoining the Club would cease, as there was a possibility that the building may be converted into swimming baths.

1892

The Committee were able to continue renting the dressing rooms in the adjoining premises.

1893

The Centre Court Stands were re-painted.

1894

An additional piece of fencing was erected on the south-west corner of the ground.

New shrubs were planted separating the ground from the railway path.

The bathing accommodation was greatly improved by the addition of three new baths, including a shower bath. Provision was made for obtaining hot water and for a drying room to be available at a total cost of £60.

1895

A new tarpaulin for use on the Centre Court was purchased at a cost of £70. The old tarpaulin was used on a second court.

1896

Croquet was played at the ground again.

1897

The Croquet Championships were resumed.

1899

The title of the Club was changed to the 'All England Lawn Tennis and Croquet Club'.

A new steel roller was purchased from Corris and Son at Epping

The accommodation of the three upper dressing rooms of the adjoining premises being inadequate, the lease was terminated and the decision taken to completely replace the old Pavilion with a new one and upgrade the Club's Dressing Rooms.

1901

A new Pavilion was opened in May, at a cost of £1,200. This gave general satisfaction to the members.

1902

The Centre Court Covered Stand B was condemned and replaced by a new structure at a cost of £255. All other stands were repaired and repainted.

In the Ladies' Dressing Room a fixed bath was provided, with a hot and cold water supply.

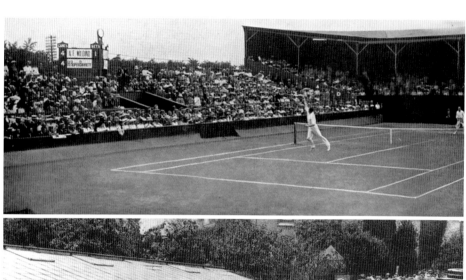

Above: 1911. A full Centre Court crowd watch a Gentlemen's singles match. Uncovered Stand D is joined to Covered Stand B. (Players – A.F. Wilding v. H.R. Barrett). Middle: 1913. The queues along Nursery Road, leading to the Club entrance, were endless to see the Gentlemen's Challenge Round. Below: 1913. At the far end of the court is the Covered Stand C, which had just been rebuilt that year. (Players – J.C. Parke v. M.E. McLoughlin – Davis Cup).

The Championships 1913. Above: A packed tea lawn in front of the Pavilion, where the caterers'
resources were taxed to the utmost. Below: Spectators queuing to gain access to the Centre Court
Uncovered Stand D. The large adjoining Covered Stand B was built in 1909 but by 1914 all three
Covered Stands were rebuilt to form a continuous structure.

1904

The Centre Court Uncovered Stand D was demolished and rebuilt to hold 600 chairs, at a total cost of £382.

Davis Cup matches were played at the ground for the first time.

The Croquet Championships were held for the last time at the ground.

Substantial improvements were made to the Pavilion, Tea Shed and Dressing Rooms.

1906

Over a period extending from the previous autumn, the three Centre Court Covered Stands, A, B and C, were demolished, rebuilt and enlarged at a total cost of £1453.

1907

No.4 and No.5 Courts were entirely re-laid and a considerable amount of re-turfing and renovation was rendered necessary around the ground by the excessive play, the previous year.

Improvements were made to the Stands and a new Tea Shed was erected. A new entrance at the railway end of the ground was provided together with increased lavatory accommodation.

A new motor mower was purchased.

A tram service from Wimbledon Station along Worple Road was started.

1908

The Olympic Games were held at the ground from 6th to 11th July.

During the autumn, the Centre Court lawn was entirely re-laid.

1909

A new and much enlarged Centre Court Covered Stand B was constructed, nine feet nearer the baseline of the court at a cost of £943. This provided an extra 500 seats, exclusive of accommodation for the Members, Committee and Press.

No.9 Court was raised five inches and re-laid.

A clock was displayed on the Centre Court for the first time.

1910

An extensive undertaking to pave and concrete paths was carried out.

No.4 Court was completely re-laid in the autumn.

1911

The Centre Court was provided with a tent-like cover, which allowed the rainwater to run into drains, especially constructed at the two sides of the court.

The old croquet summer houses, which had been a feature of the Club for so many years, were overhauled and renovated.

Tar paths were laid down in front of the Pavilion, Dressing Rooms and Tea Shed, also from the main Entrance Gates to Centre Court Covered Stands A, B and C.

In the autumn, No.5 Court was completely re-laid and the whole of the stands, boundary fence and Tea-Shed were re-painted.

1912

Considerable improvements were carried out. Tar paving was laid down around the Centre Court and a new lavatory erected at the Railway Entrance Gate to the ground.

In the autumn, No.6, No.7 and No.8 Courts were completely re-laid and numerous surface drains placed in various parts of the ground.

1913

'The World's Championships on Grass' was added to the traditional title of The Championships, as a result of the International Lawn Tennis Federation awarding this title to the British Isles in perpetuity. As a consequence, Ladies' Doubles and Mixed Doubles Championships were added to the programme.

A new and enlarged Centre Court Covered Stand C was constructed, at a cost of £1,019, giving additional accommodation for over 400 people. Uncovered Stand D was condemned as unsafe for further use and rebuilt at a cost of £560.

At the rear of Stand C a new tar path was laid down.

The fence at the south-west side of the ground was renewed.

A new motor roller was purchased.

Two houses adjoining the ground (No.108 and No.110 Worple Road) were purchased by the Club in the autumn at a cost of £2,404. The gardens of these premises were opened with access to the ground.

A special tram service was started between Wimbledon Station and the ground.

1914

A new and much enlarged Centre Court Covered Stand A, with passage way underneath overlooking No.1 and No.2 Courts, was constructed at a cost of £1,806. This stand, which was joined as a continuous structure to Stands B and C, increased the seating capacity of the court from 2,300 to 3,500.

The two houses in Worple Road adjoining the ground were converted into accommodation for lady members, competitors during The Championships and a Club Office. The gardens were converted into a new Tea Lawn, while the Tea Sheds were removed from near the Main Entrance Gate to the terraces of the houses.

Additional tar-paved paths were laid down.

1915-1918

The Championships were suspended during the First World War.

All expenditure was strictly confined to items necessary to maintaining the ground in a reasonable condition.

Towards the end of the War, donations from members and well-wishers enabled the Club to survive.

Many improvements were made to the Worple Road ground in 1914. Above: The new Centre Court Covered Stand A, which increased the seating capacity of the court from 2,300 to 3,500. Middle: The covered passageway, underneath the new Stand A, which overlooked No. 1 and No. 2 Courts. Below: The new Tea Lawn occupying the gardens of the newly purchased two houses in Worple Road, looking down to the ground, with the new Stand A in the background.

1914. Above: Looking out from the ground through the main turnstiles into Nursery Road, which led up to Worple Road. The building on the right was occupied by the Dressing Rooms and further along were the Secretary's Office and Pavilion. Below: The ground side of the turnstiles showing spectators watching a match on No. 4 Court with the building in the distance being the railway entrance to the ground. On the extreme right is the Centre Court.

1919
The Championships were resumed.

An uncovered Stand was erected at the side of No.4 Court.

1920
Because of lack of space at the ground, the Club decided to move to larger premises and purchased land at Wimbledon Park in preparation for the opening of a new ground at Wimbledon Park Road (later Church Road) in 1922. Consequently, expenditure towards ground improvements were kept at a minimum for two years.

1921
After 41 meetings The Championships were played at Worple Road for the final time. The last ball was hit by Suzanne Lenglen on the Centre Court.

Layout of Courts

1877–1880 [12]   1881–1921 [10]

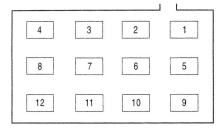 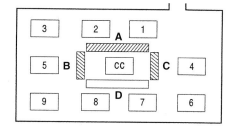

Construction of Centre Court Stands

Stand	Temporary	Permanent
A (Covered)	1881	1884, 1906, 1914
B (Covered)	1881	1885, 1902, 1906, 1909
C (Covered)	1881	1885, 1906, 1913
D (Uncovered)	–	1886, 1904, 1913

Centre Court Seat Prices

| Year | Reserved seat in covered stands | |
	Whole meeting (1)	Daily (2)
1880	7s.6d.	First week – 1s.0d., Second week – 2s.6d.
1881–1890	10s.0d.	—
1891	10s.6d.	—
1892–1894	5s.0d., 7s.6d., and 10s.0d.	From 1s.0d.
1895	7s.6d. and 10s.0d.	From 1s.0d.
1896–1897	7s.6d. and 10s.6d.	From 1s.0d.
1898–1903	7s.6d. and 10s.6d.	1s.0d., 2s.6d., and 5s.0d.
1904	7s.6d.	2s.6d.
1905–1907	17s.6d.	—
1908–1912	£1.1s.0d.	—
1913	£1.1s.0d.	2s.0d. and 3s.0d.
1914	£1.11s.6d.	—
1919–1921	£1.15s.0d.	3s.6d.

Notes: 1. From 1883 to 1904 the price did not include ground admission.
From 1905 to 1921 the price did include ground admission.
2. The price did not include ground admission.

Ground Admission

Year	Whole meeting	Daily
1877–1878	—	1s.0d.
1879–1880	5s.0d.	1s.0d.
1881–1882	7s.6d.	First five days – 1s.0d. After – 2s.6d.
1883	7s.6d.	1s.0d. Last five days –2s.6d.
1884	12s.6d.	1s.0d. Final – 2s.0d.
1885–1886	12s.6d.	First three days – 1s.0d. After – 2s.6d.
1887–1888	7s.6d.	1s.0d. Finals – 2s.6d.
1889–1890	10s.0d.	1s.0d. Finals – 2s.6d.
1891	10s.0d.	1s.0d. Semi-finals and Finals – 2s.6d.
1892–1895	7s.6d.	First three days – 1s.0d. After – 2s.6d.
1896–1904	7s.6d.	First day – 1s.0d. After – 2s.6d.
1905–1908	7s.6d.	2s.6d.
1909–1913	10s.0d.	2s.6d.
1914	15s.0d.	2s.6d.
1919–1921	17s.6d.	3s.0d.

Profits from Lawn Tennis Championship Meetings

Year	Profit	Year	Profit	Year	Profit
1877	-	1891	£256	1905	£2104
1878	-	1892	£318	1906	£2263
1879	£116	1893	£270	1907	£1268
1880	£306	1894	£218	1908	£1165
1881	£541	1895	–£33	1909	£1103
1882	£344	1896	£142	1910	£1760
1883	£426	1897	£132	1911	£2401
1884	£614	1898	£70	1912	£2293
1885	£797	1899	£200	1913	£3518
1886	£535	1900	£311	1914	£5741
1887	£276	1901	£735	1919	£6769
1888	£530	1902	£548	1920	£6430
1889	£436	1903	£780	1921	£5679
1890	£321	1904	£1,291		

Two aerial views of the ground in 1921, the last occasion when The Championships were held at Worple Road, before moving to Wimbledon Park. The open fields that surrounded the ground 50 years earlier, had become completely built up. The photographs show why it was so easy for the ground to be packed to suffocation at times, particularly when, at the end of play, the Centre Court crowd turned out and tried to negotiate the very narrow paths around the outer courts.

Miscellany

Nursery Road
Nursery Road, led down from Worple Road to the entrance to the Club and took its name from the Worple Nursery, which was established on the west side from around 1880. The business was run from the corner house in Worple Road by George Legg, and later his son Ernest, and had a large greenhouse and a line of greenhouses in the garden behind. After changing hands several times, the premises finally closed in 1938. From 1965 to date the site has been used as an Ambulance Station.

Covered Courts
In the late 1870s a roller skating rink was erected on the east side of Nursery Road, just before the main entrance to the Club, and to the rear of the Club Pavilion. Interest in this pastime waned quickly and in 1880 the whole rink was offered to the Club for use on weekdays, but this was not accepted. However, five Members of the Club, led by F.W. Oliver, purchased the premises and converted it into two covered courts (a singles court and a doubles court). Gradually the use of the courts declined and by the early 1890s they became disused. The floor of black asphalt was most satisfactory but there was little room to spare at the back and sides of the courts, and the ceiling was too low.

There was the possibility in 1891 of the building being converted into a swimming bath, but nothing came of this. A year later a Catholic Boys' School took possession of the premises to provide extra space for their rising numbers but their occupation lasted only about a year. Then a 'Rocket Cycle and Riding School' took out a lease for a while, and eventually the premises were converted for use as a factory.

Since then the area was used for housing and various commercial activities but in 1995 the existing two buildings were demolished and a 24 apartment block built, known as Pavilion Court.

From 1880 the Club annually rented the three upper dressing rooms in the building to augment the accommodation available during The Championships but these were no longer required after 1900, as a new and larger Pavilion was built to replace the old one and the Club Dressing Rooms were enlarged and re-arranged.

Suffragettes
On the night of 26th February 1913, suffragettes attempted to set fire to the Centre Court Stands and damage the lawns at the Worple Road ground.

Fortunately an alert night watchman spotted the intruders who were just about to set fire to the wooden Stand B. He chased one of the ladies, who fell over some building material in the dark before capturing and escorting her to the Pavilion to await the arrival of the police. Later in the year, at The Championships, there were minor demonstrations outside the ground and spectators arriving carrying bags or parcels underwent scrutiny or a search by the attendants.

Groundsmen

The Coleman family served the Club well as groundsmen for over 50 years. Thomas Coleman was appointed in 1888 and, when he died in 1907, was succeeded by his son William, who remained in the post until 1938. Other members of the Coleman family also served at the ground.

Dressing Room Attendant

John Wilson served as Dressing Room Attendant at the Club from the late 1870s to 1907. In the early days he was also manager of the adjoining covered courts. This instantly recognisable man, with full beard, lived on to 1915 when he died at the age of 91.

Croquet Champions

Year	Croquet Champions		Club Champions	
1869*	G.C. Joad	–	W.H. Peel	Mrs. G.C. Joad
1870	W.H. Peel	–	J.D. Heath	Miss Walter
1871	W.H. Peel	Mrs. J.H. Walsh	J.D. Heath	Mrs. J.H. Walsh
1872	C. Black	Mrs. J.H. Walsh	A. Law	Mrs. J. Holmes
1873	J.D. Heath	Mrs. J.H. Walsh	J.D. Heath	Miss C.L. Walsh
1874	J.D. Heath	Miss Williamson	J.D. Heath	Mrs. Hallowes
1875	R. Gray	Mrs. Hallowes	R. Gray	Miss C.L. Walsh
1876	Col. Busk	Miss K. Philbrick	H. Jones	–
1877	B.C. Evelegh	Miss K. Philbrick	B.C. Evelegh	Mrs. Davidson
1878	A.H.E. Spong	Miss Walsh	B.C. Evelegh	Miss Walsh
1879	B.C. Evelegh	Miss Walsh	A.H.E. Spong	Miss Walsh
1880	A.H.E. Spong	Miss Walsh	B.C. Evelegh	Miss Walsh
1881	A.H.E. Spong	Miss K. Philbrick	–	–
1882	A.H.E. Spong	–	–	–
1897	C.E. Willis	Miss M. Drummond	–	–
1898	Rev. C. Powell	Miss O. Henry	–	–
1899	B.C. Evelegh	Miss L. Gower	C.E. Willis	Miss L. Gower
1900	J.E. Austin	Miss L. Gower	C.E. Willis	Mrs. W. Whittaker
1901	R.N. Roper	Miss L. Gower	W.W. Bruce	Miss Fawcett
1902	C. Corbally	Miss M. Glyn	A.G.A. Clark	Mrs. W. Whittaker
1903	C. Corbally	Miss N. Coote	C.E. Willis	Miss Cowie
1904	R.C.J. Beaton	Miss V. Rowley	H.H. Minton	Miss A. Jones

*Played at Crystal Palace.

Lawn Tennis Champions

Year	Gentlemen's Singles	Ladies' Singles	Gentlemen's Doubles
1877	S.W. Gore	-	-
1878	P.F. Hadow	-	-
1879	J.T. Hartley	-	-
1880	J.T. Hartley	-	-
1881	W.C. Renshaw	-	-
1882	W.C. Renshaw	-	-
1883	W.C. Renshaw	-	-
1884	W.C. Renshaw	Miss M.E. Watson	J.E. Renshaw and W.C. Renshaw
1885	W.C. Renshaw	Miss M.E. Watson	J.E. Renshaw and W.C. Renshaw
1886	W.C. Renshaw	Miss B. Bingley	J.E. Renshaw and W.C. Renshaw
1887	H.F. Lawford	Miss C. Dod	P.B. Lyon and H.W.W. Wilberforce
1888	J.E. Renshaw	Miss C. Dod	J.E. Renshaw and W.C. Renshaw
1889	W.C. Renshaw	Mrs. G.W. Hillyard	J.E. Renshaw andW.C. Renshaw
1890	W.J. Hamilton	Miss H.G.B. Rice	J. Pim and F.O. Stoker
1891	W. Baddeley	Miss C. Dod	H. Baddeley and W. Baddeley
1892	W. Baddeley	Miss C. Dod	H.S. Barlow and E.W. Lewis
1893	J. Pim	Miss C. Dod	J. Pim and F.O. Stoker
1894	J. Pim	Mrs. G.W. Hillyard	H. Baddeley and W. Baddeley
1895	W. Baddeley	Miss C.R. Cooper	H. Baddeley and W. Baddeley
1896	H.S. Mahony	Miss C.R. Cooper	H. Baddeley and W. Baddeley
1897	R.F. Doherty	Mrs. G.W. Hillyard	H.L. Doherty and R.F. Doherty
1898	R.F. Doherty	Miss C.R. Cooper	H.L. Doherty and R.F. Doherty
1899	R.F. Doherty	Mrs. G.W. Hillyard	H.L. Doherty and R.F. Doherty
1900	R.F. Doherty	Mrs. G.W. Hillyard	H.L. Doherty and R.F. Doherty
1901	A.W. Gore	Mrs. A. Sterry	H.L. Doherty and R.F. Doherty
1902	H.L. Doherty	Miss M.E. Robb	F.L. Riseley and S.H. Smith
1903	H.L. Doherty	Miss D.K. Douglass	H.L. Doherty and R.F. Doherty
1904	H.L. Doherty	Miss D.K. Douglass	H.L. Doherty and R.F. Doherty
1905	H.L. Doherty	Miss M.G. Sutton	H.L. Doherty and R.F. Doherty
1906	H.L. Doherty	Miss D.K. Douglass	F.L. Riseley and S.H. Smith
1907	N.E. Brookes	Miss M.G. Sutton	N.E. Brookes and A.F. Wilding
1908	A.W. Gore	Mrs. A. Sterry	M.J.G. Ritchie and A.F. Wilding
1909	A.W. Gore	Miss P.D.H. Boothby	H.R. Barrett and A.W. Gore
1910	A.F. Wilding	Mrs. R.L. Chambers	M.J.G. Ritchie and A.F. Wilding
1911	A.F. Wilding	Mrs. R.L. Chambers	M.O. Decugis and A.H. Gobert
1912	A.F. Wilding	Mrs. D.T.R. Larcombe	H.R. Barrett and C.P. Dixon
1913	A.F. Wilding	Mrs. R.L. Chambers	H.R. Barrett and C.P. Dixon
1914	N.E. Brookes	Mrs. R.L. Chambers	N.E. Brookes and A.F. Wilding
1919	G.L. Patterson	Miss S.R.F. Lenglen	R.V. Thomas and P.O. Wood
1920	W.T. Tilden	Miss S.R.F. Lenglen	C.S. Garland and R.N. Williams
1921	W.T. Tilden	Miss S.R.F. Lenglen	R. Lycett and M. Woosnam

Year	Ladies' Doubles	Mixed Doubles
1913	Miss P.D.H. Boothby and Mrs. J.R. McNair	H. Crisp and Mrs. C.O. Tuckey
1914	Miss A.M. Morton and Miss E.M. Ryan	J.C. Parke and Mrs. D.T.R. Larcombe
1919	Miss S.R.F. Lenglen and Miss E.M. Ryan	R. Lycett and Miss E.M. Ryan
1920	Miss S.R.F. Lenglen and Miss E.M. Ryan	G.L. Patterson and Miss S.R.F. Lenglen
1921	Miss S.R.F. Lenglen and Miss E.M. Ryan	R. Lycett and Miss E.M. Ryan

Officers of the Club

Patron
1910–1936   H.M. King George V

Presidents
1869–1874	The Earl of Essex	1912-1915	The Lord Desborough, KCVO
1907-1910	H.R.H. Prince of Wales	1915-1921	H. Wilson Fox, MP
1911-1912	A.W. Gore	1921-1929	H.W.W. Wilberforce

Vice-Presidents
1869–1874	E. Marjoribanks	1911-1921	H.W.W. Wilberforce
1911-1919	H.L. Doherty	1914-1921	W.H. Collins
1911-1923	R.B. Hough	1915-1945	The Rt. Hon. Lord
1911-1915	D. Jones		Desborough, KG GCVO

Secretaries
1868-1869	W.J. Whitmore
1869	E.B. Mitchell
1869-1871	S.H.C. Maddock
1871	H. Jones
1871-1879	J.H. Walsh
1880-1888	J. Marshall
1888-1891	H.W.W. Wilberforce
1891-1898	A.J. Chitty
1899-1906	A. Palmer
1907-1925*	Com. G.W. Hillyard

Hon. Treasurers
1868-1869	S.H.C. Maddock
1869-1875	J.H. Walsh
1875-1882	Rev. D.I. Heath
1882-1886	F.W. Oliver
1886-1898	A.J. Chitty
1899-1909	A. Palmer
1910-1937	C.A. Caridia

*From November 1914 to May 1919, C.A. Caridia was Acting Hon. Secretary while the Secretary was on active service.

Companion books – 'Wimbledon 1922. The New Ground and Centre Court'.
'Wimbledon 1922–2014. The Changing Face of Church Road'.

Published by
Wimbledon Lawn Tennis Museum, All England Lawn Tennis Club, Church Road, Wimbledon, London SW19 5AE.
Third Edition of 2003

© Alan Little and Wimbledon Lawn Tennis Museum.

ISBN 978 0 906741 58 0

The author thanks Audrey Snell, Asst. Librarian at the Wimbledon Lawn Tennis Museum, for her assistance with the production.

Printed by Remous Ltd, Milborne Port, Sherborne, Dorset DT9 5EP.